I'm Good At

I'm Good at Making Art

Eileen M. Day

Heinemann Library

Chicago, Illinois

Customer Service 888-454-2279
Visit our website at www.heinemannlibrary.com

Designed by Sue Emerson, Heinemann Library; Page layout by Que-Net Media
Printed and bound in the United States by Lake Book Manufacturing, Inc.
Photo research by Alan Gottlieb and Amor Montes de Oca

07 06 05 04 03
10 9 8 7 6 5 4 3 2 1

Library of Congress Cataloging-in-Publication Data
Day, Eileen.
   I'm good at making art / Eileen Day.
       p. cm. – (I'm good at)
Includes index.
Summary: Explains what art is and how it feels to make art, and discusses different types of art, such as painting, drawing, origami, and pottery.
   ISBN 1-4034-0898-X (HC), 1-4034-3446-8 (Pbk.)
1. Art–Technique–Juvenile literature. [1. Art–Technique. 2. Handicraft.] I. Title. II. Series: Day, Eileen.   I'm good at.
   N7440 .D39 2003
   372.5–dc21

                                          2002014732

Acknowledgments
The author and publishers are grateful to the following for permission to reproduce copyrighted material:
p. 4 Ellen Senisi/The Image Works; p. 5 Jose Luis Pelaez, Inc./Corbis; pp. 6, 7, 10, 11, 12, 13, 14, 15, 16, 17, 20, 21, 22, 23 (row 1) 24, back cover Robert Lifson/Heinemann Library; pp. 8, 9 Jennie Woocock/Reflections Photolibrary/Corbis; pp. 18, 19 Greg Williams/Heinemann Library; p. 23 (row 2, L-R) Jose Luis Pelaez, Inc./Corbis, Robert Lifson/Heinemann Library, Robert Lifson/Heinemann Library; p. 23 (row 3, L-R) Brand X Pictures, Greg Williams/Heinemann Library

Cover photograph by Jose Luis Pelaez, Inc./Corbis

Every effort has been made to contact copyright holders of any material reproduced in this book. Any omissions will be rectified in subsequent printings if notice is given to the publisher.

Special thanks to our advisory panel for their help in the preparation of this book:

Alice Bethke,
Library Consultant
Palo Alto, CA

Kathleen Gilbert,
Second Grade Teacher
Round Rock, TX

Sandra Gilbert,
Library Media Specialist
Fiest Elementary School
Houston, TX

Jan Gobeille,
Kindergarten Teacher
Garfield Elementary
Oakland, CA

Angela Leeper,
Educational Consultant
North Carolina Department
of Public Instruction
Wake Forest, NC

Special thanks to the Evanston Art Center for allowing us to photograph in their studio.

Some words are shown in bold, **like this.**
You can find them in the picture glossary on page 23.

Contents

What Is Making Art?

Making art is making something nice to look at.

People who make art use their imaginations.

People who make art are called **artists.**

When I make art, I am being creative.

What Is Drawing?

crayons

pencils

chalk

When I draw, I make a picture of something.

I can draw with pencils, crayons, and **chalk**.

Sometimes I draw what I see.

Sometimes I draw what I feel inside.

What Is Painting?

paint brush

paint

When I paint, I make a picture with colors.

Sometimes I use paints and a brush.

I can paint pictures with my fingers.

Finger paints feel gooey.

What Is Origami?

Origami is a special way of folding paper.

I can use any color of paper.

I fold the paper many times.

Then the paper is in the shape of a bird.

What Is Adinkra Stamping?

Adinkra stamping is putting designs on cloth or paper.

I push the stamp into some ink.

Then I put the stamp on a piece of cloth.

It makes a pattern.

What Is Weaving?

When I **weave,** I put together strips of paper.

The strips fit together tightly.

I weave the strips over and under.

I can make a mat.

What Is Collage?

tissue paper

Collage is a picture made from pieces of things.

We can make a collage with **tissue paper.**

We paste down the tissue paper.

It makes a design.

What Is Pottery?

Pottery is making things with clay.

First, the clay is soft and squishy.

Then, I squeeze the clay into
a shape.

When the clay dries, I have a bowl.

How Do I Feel When I Make Art?

When I make art, I feel proud.

I know I can make it by myself.

Making art makes me happy.

I can make art every day.

Quiz

What do you need to make these things?

Look for the answers on page 24.

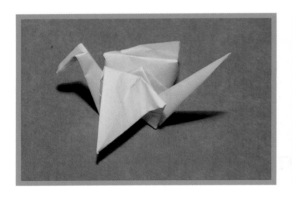

Picture Glossary

Adinkra stamping
pages 12–13

**collage
(ka-läzh)**
page 16

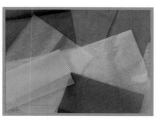

tissue paper
pages 16, 17

artist
page 5

origami
pages 10–11

weave
pages 14–15

chalk
page 6

pottery
pages 18–19

Note to Parents and Teachers

Reading for information is an important part of a child's literacy development. Learning begins with a question about something. Help children think of themselves as investigators and researchers by encouraging their questions about the world around them. Each chapter in this book begins with a question. Read the question together. Look at the pictures. Talk about what you think the answer might be. Then read the text to find out if your predictions were correct. Think of other questions you could ask about the topic, and discuss where you might find the answers. Assist children in using the picture glossary and the index to practice new vocabulary and research skills.

Index

Answers to quiz on page 22

You use **tissue paper** and glue to make a **collage**.

You use color paper to make an **origami** bird.